Animal Life Cycles

Kate Boehm Jerome

PICTURE CREDITS

Cover (front), 9 (top right), 24, 31 (top right), 32 Photodisc Green/Getty Images; 1 Anthony Bannister, Gallo Images/Corbis; 2-3, 4-5 (top) Stone/Getty Images; 4-5 (bottom) Jeff Daly/Visuals Unlimited; 5 (top) Michael Redmer/Visuals Unlimited; 5 (bottom), 6-7, 17, 31 (top left), 34 (middle), 35 (bottom), 36 The Image Bank/Getty Images; 7 (top) William Dow/Corbis; 7 (middle) Tom Brakefield/Corbis; 7 (bottom); Alissa Crandal/Corbis; 8, 35 (top) Terry W. Eggers/Corbis; 9 (top middle), 31 (bottom left and bottom right) D. Robert & Lorri Franz/Corbis; 9 (top left) Theo Allofs/Corbis; 9 (bottom) Image Library 1000/Ingram Publishing; 10 Steve Winter/National Geographic Image Collection; 11 (top middle and top right), 34 (second from bottom) George Grall/National Geographic Image Collection; 11 (top left), 34 (top) Gary Meszaros/www.bciusa.com; 11 (bottom) Lynda Richardson/Corbis; 12 Art Wolfe/ Photo Researchers, Inc.; 13 (top middle), 34 (bottom) D. Lyones/www.bciusa.com; 13 (top left), 34 (bottom) Raymond Coleman/Visuals Unlimited; 13 (top right), 34 (bottom) Bob Grossington/ www.bciusa.com; 13 (bottom) Gary Meszaros/Visuals Unlimited; 14 Michael & Patricia Fogden/Corbis; 15 (top middle); John Visser/ www.bciusa.com; 15 (top left) Daniel Zupanc/ www.bciusa.com; 15 (top right) Wolfgang Bayer/www.bciusa.com; 15 (bottom) Craig Lovell/Corbis; 16 (left) Patrice Ricard/www.bciusa.com; 16 (right) Photographer's Choice/Getty Images; 18-19 Tim Davis/Corbis; 20, 23 (middle), 34 (second from top) David Cavagnaro/Visuals Unlimited; 21, 30 (bottom right) Kim Taylor/www.bciusa.com; 22, 23 (left), 30 (top right) Royalty-Free/ Corbis; 23 (right) Gary W. Carter/Corbis; 25 (left) Jason Edwards/ National Geographic Image Collection; 25 (top) Ron Boardman, Frank Lane Picture Agency/Corbis; 25 (right) Jane Burton/www.bciusa.com; 26 (left, middle, and right) Rubberball Productions/ Getty Images; 27 (top) Taxi/Getty Images; 27 (bottom) Digital Vision/Getty Images;

28 Charles Philip Cangialosi/Corbis; 29, 30 (bottom left) Brandon D. Cole/Corbis; 30 (top left) Brand X Pictures/Getty Images; 31 (middle left) Medford Taylor/ National Geographic Image Collection; 31 (middle right) George H. H. Huey/Corbis; 35 (second from top) A. Blank/www.bciusa.com; 35 (second from bottom) Bianca Lavies/National Geographic Image Collection.

Produced through the worldwide resources of the National Geographic Society, John M. Fahey, Jr., President and Chief Executive Officer; Gilbert M. Grosvenor, Chairman of the Board; Nina D. Hoffman, Executive Vice President and President, Books and Education Publishing Group.

PREPARED BY NATIONAL GEOGRAPHIC SCHOOL PUBLISHING

Ericka Markman, Senior Vice President and President, Children's Books and Education Publishing Group; Steve Mico, Senior Vice President, Editorial Director, Publisher; Francis Downey, Executive Editor; Richard Easby, Editorial Manager; Bea Jackson, Director of Layout and Design; Jim Hiscott, Design Manager; Cynthia Olson, Art Director; Margaret Sidlosky, Illustrations Director; Matt Wascavage, Manager of Publishing Services; Sean Philpotts, Jane Ponton, Production Managers; Ted Tucker, Production Specialist.

MANUFACTURING AND QUALITY CONTROL

Christopher A. Liedel, Chief Financial Officer; Phillip L. Schlosser, Director; Clifton M. Brown III, Manager

BOOK DEVELOPMENT

Amy Sarver

◀ These highland cows grow and change during their lives.

Contents

CONSULTANT AND REVIEWER
Kefyn M. Catley, Ph.D., Assistant Professor of Science Education, Department of
Teaching and Learning, Peabody College; Assistant Professor of Biology, Vanderbilt
University; Research Associate, Division of Invertebrate Zoology, American Museum of
Natural History, New York

BOOK DESIGN/PHOTO RESEARCH
3R1 Group, Inc.

Published by the National Geographic Society
1145 17th Street N.W.
Washington, D.C. 20036-4688

ISBN-13: 978-0-7922-5305-1
ISBN-10: 0-7922-5305-1
2012
   3 4 5 6 7 8 9 10 11 12 13 14 15

Printed in Canada.

Groups of Animals

▲ Orangutans are mammals.

Earth is home to many kinds of animals. Different animals are grouped together because they have features in common. Some groups of animals are

- mammals,
- amphibians,
- insects, and
- reptiles.

All animals have one feature that they share. They all change as they grow.

▲ Bees are insects.

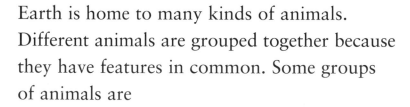

▲ Frogs are amphibians.

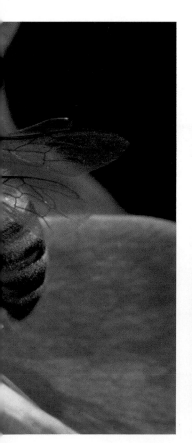

▲ Snakes are reptiles.

5

Big Idea
Animals grow and change throughout their lives.

Set Purpose
Learn about the life cycles of different kinds of animals.

Questions You Will Explore

How do animals change during their life cycles?

How do the life cycles of different kinds of animals compare?

Animal Life Cycles

Animals change during their lives. These changes are part of an animal's **life cycle**. A life cycle is the stages an animal goes through during its life. All animal life cycles are the same in some ways:

- Animals begin life.
- Animals grow and change.
- Animals have young.

In this book, you will learn about life cycles of different kinds of animals.

....

life cycle – the stages an animal goes through during its life

Begin life

Grow and change

Have young

▲ These horses are mammals.

Life Cycle of a Mammal

Mammals are one group of animals. Mammals change during their life cycles. Most mammals give birth to live babies. The babies often look a lot like their parents. Mammals grow and change as they get older. Adult mammals have babies. Then the mammal life cycle starts over again.

Mammal Features

- **Have backbones**
- **Feed their babies milk**
- **Often have hair or fur**

....
mammal – a kind of animal that has a backbone, feeds its young milk, and is usually covered with hair

Life Cycle of a Tiger

A baby tiger grows and becomes a young tiger.

A young tiger grows and becomes an adult tiger.

An adult tiger mates to make baby tigers.

A Tiger's Life Cycle

Let's look at the life cycle of one mammal—the tiger. Baby tigers are small. They look a lot like their parents. Baby tigers drink their mother's milk for a few months. Then the young tigers begin to hunt for food with their mother.

▼ Tiger

The tiger grows and changes as it gets older. Its body gets larger. It becomes an adult. Adult tigers can **mate,** or make babies. The female tiger gives birth to babies. The tiger life cycle begins again.

....
mate – to make babies

9

▲ This frog is an amphibian.

Life Cycle of an Amphibian

Amphibians are another group of animals. Amphibians change during their life cycles. Many start life as eggs laid in water. The eggs hatch and become **larvae**. The larvae live in the water and breathe through gills. Gills let the amphibians breathe underwater. Then the larvae change and become adults. Some adult amphibians have lungs. Lungs let the amphibians breathe air and live on land. Adult amphibians mate, and the life cycle begins again.

Amphibian Features

- Have backbones
- Live part of life in water
- Often live part of life on land

amphibian – animal that often lives part of its life on land and part in water

larva – an early stage in the life of an amphibian or other kind of animal

10

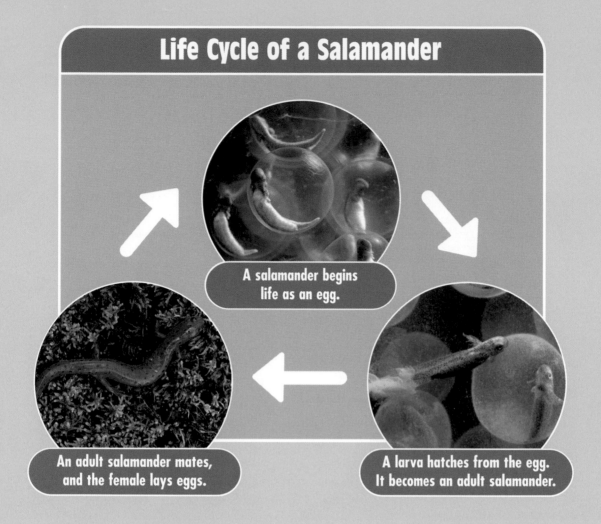

Life Cycle of a Salamander

A salamander begins life as an egg.

A larva hatches from the egg. It becomes an adult salamander.

An adult salamander mates, and the female lays eggs.

A Salamander's Life Cycle

Let's look at the life cycle of one amphibian—the salamander. Some kinds of salamanders begin life as eggs. The eggs hatch into larvae that look like little fish. Soon they change. They grow legs. Some salamanders use lungs to breathe air. The salamanders become adults.

Adult salamanders mate. Female salamanders lay eggs. Some lay thousands of eggs! Then the life cycle of the salamanders starts over again.

▼ Salamander

11

▲ This dragonfly is an insect with three stages in its life cycle.

Life Cycle of an Insect

Insects are another group of animals. Insects have different life cycles. Some insects have three life cycle stages. Others have four life cycle stages. All insects begin life as eggs. An insect with three life cycle stages then changes to a **nymph.** Nymphs look like adults, but they usually do not have wings. The nymphs shed their skin several times. Then they become adults that can mate.

Insect Features

- **Hard outer covering**
- **Six legs**
- **Three body parts**

....

insect – animal that has six legs, three body parts, and a hard outer covering

nymph – a stage in the life of some insects between egg and adult

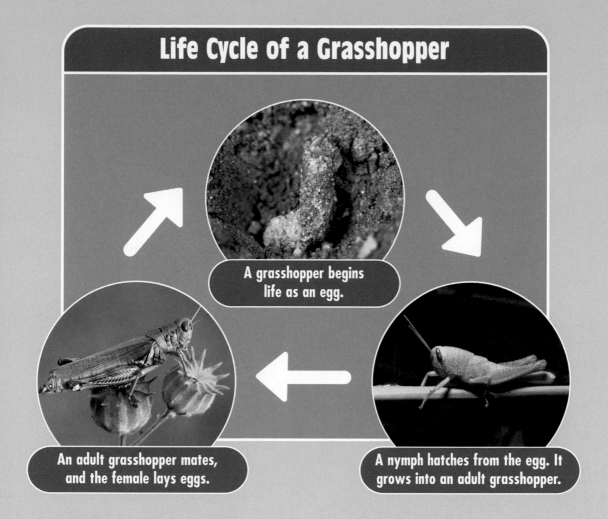

Life Cycle of a Grasshopper

A grasshopper begins life as an egg.

A nymph hatches from the egg. It grows into an adult grasshopper.

An adult grasshopper mates, and the female lays eggs.

A Grasshopper's Life Cycle

Grasshoppers are insects. They have three stages in their life cycles. A grasshopper starts life as an egg. When the egg hatches, a nymph crawls out. The nymph does not have wings. The nymph grows for 40 to 60 days. It sheds its skin many times. Then it becomes an adult. The adult grasshopper has wings and can fly to find a mate.

Adult grasshoppers mate. Some female grasshoppers can lay more than one hundred eggs. Then the grasshopper life cycle begins again.

▼ Grasshopper

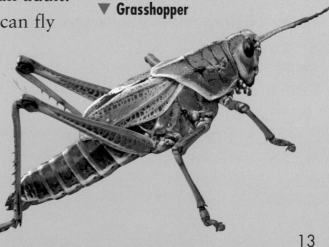

13

▲ This chameleon is a reptile.

Life Cycle of a Reptile

Reptiles are another group of animals. Reptiles change during their life cycles. Many reptiles lay eggs. Other kinds of reptiles give birth to live young that look like their parents. The young reptiles grow and change. They get larger and become adults. Adult reptiles can mate. Then the life cycle begins again.

....

reptile – animal that has a backbone and scales, and uses the sun or warm surfaces to heat its body

Reptile Features

- **Have backbones**

- **Have scales**

- **Depend on the sun or warm surfaces to heat their bodies**

Life Cycle of a Crocodile

A crocodile begins life as an egg.

A young crocodile hatches from an egg. It becomes an adult crocodile.

An adult crocodile mates, and the female lays eggs.

A Crocodile's Life Cycle

Crocodiles are reptiles. A mother crocodile lays eggs. She keeps these eggs in a nest. After two or three months, the eggs hatch. The young crocodiles crawl from their nest. They grow and change. They get larger and become adults.

Adult crocodiles mate. After a few weeks, the female lays her eggs. Then the crocodile life cycle begins again.

▼ Crocodile

▼ Bird

▼ Fish

Many Groups of Animals

You have learned about mammals, amphibians, insects, and reptiles. These are just some animal groups. There are other groups of animals, such as birds and fish.

Animals in each group often have similar life cycles. For example, most mammals give birth to live babies. Most amphibians lay eggs in water.

▲ During their lives, animals grow and change.

Life Cycles of All Animals

Each group of animals may have a special life cycle. But all animal life cycles have some things in common. Animals are born. They grow and change. They mate and make more of their own kind. Animals die.

Every time a new animal is born, the life cycle begins again. This is how the cycle of life keeps going for all animals.

Stop and Think!

HOW does one kind of animal change during its life cycle?

Recap

Explain how an animal changes during its life cycle.

Set Purpose

Learn about the life cycle of a praying mantis.

Life as a
Prayin

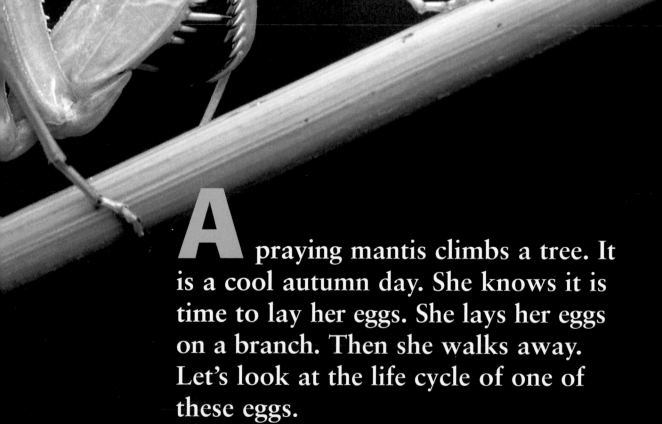

g Mantis

A praying mantis climbs a tree. It is a cool autumn day. She knows it is time to lay her eggs. She lays her eggs on a branch. Then she walks away. Let's look at the life cycle of one of these eggs.

Egg case

▲ An egg case protects praying mantis eggs.

An Egg

A praying mantis is an insect. It has three stages in its life cycle. It begins life as an egg. The female mantis lays eggs in autumn. She may lay hundreds of eggs. Then she leaves. Many of the eggs do not survive. Some eggs are eaten by other animals.

Mantis eggs do not hatch until spring. How do they survive a cold winter? The eggs are held together in an **egg case**. The egg case is a hard covering that protects the eggs.

....

egg case – a hard covering that protects eggs

A Nymph

In spring, the weather gets warmer. The praying mantis egg hatches. The young praying mantis looks like a small adult. It is called a nymph. Hundreds of other nymphs are also coming out of the egg case. They are climbing on top of one another. They are everywhere!

The nymph walks away from the others. It searches for food. Over time, the nymph grows bigger. It sheds its skin many times.

Nymph

◀ Praying mantis nymphs hatch from eggs in an egg case.

An Adult

By the end of the summer, the praying mantis is fully grown. It is now an adult. It is several inches long and has wings. It flies and finds other praying mantises. Soon the praying mantis mates.

The praying mantis mates in autumn. After mating, the female lays eggs. She lays eggs six times. After laying her last eggs, the female dies.

▼ A female praying mantis lays eggs.

Life Cycle of a Praying Mantis

A praying mantis begins life as an egg.

A nymph hatches from the egg. It becomes an adult praying mantis.

An adult praying mantis mates, and the female lays eggs.

The life cycle of a praying mantis does not stop. The female dies. Yet many of her eggs survive. The eggs will hatch. Many nymphs will crawl out of their egg case. These new praying mantises will grow and change. Then the adults will mate. The praying mantis life cycle begins again.

Stop and Think!

HOW does a praying mantis change during its life cycle?

Recap

Explain how a praying mantis changes during its life cycle.

Set Purpose

Read these articles to find out more about animals and their life cycles.

CONNECT WHAT YOU HAVE LEARNED

Animal Life Cycles

All animals change as they get older. The changes that an animal goes through during its life are called a life cycle.

Here are some ideas you learned about animal life cycles:

- All animals are born.
- Animals grow and change as they get older.
- Adult animals can have babies.
- When an adult has babies, the life cycle begins again.

Check What You Have Learned

HOW is the life cycle of this frog like the life cycle of a salamander?

Life Cycle of a Frog

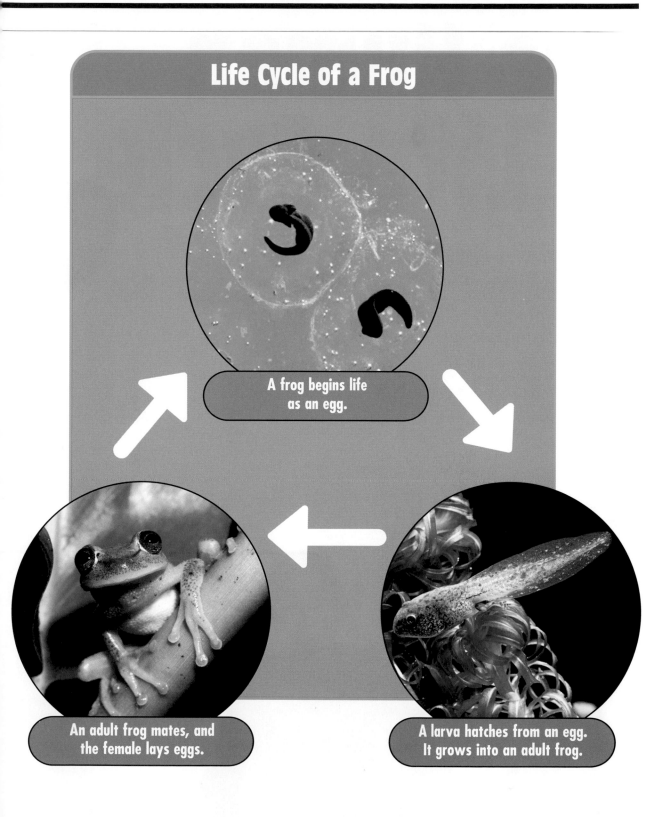

A frog begins life as an egg.

A larva hatches from an egg. It grows into an adult frog.

An adult frog mates, and the female lays eggs.

The Human Life Cycle

Did you know that people have life cycles, too? Humans are mammals. So human life cycles are similar to those of other mammals. Human mothers give birth to live babies. The babies grow and change. They get larger. They become adults. Adults can mate and have babies. Then the human life cycle begins again.

▼ People grow and change during their lives.

Heavy and Tall

▼ A baby elephant can weigh more than 100 kilograms (224 pounds).

Elephants are mammals. They have the heaviest babies on land. A baby elephant can weigh more than 100 kilograms (224 pounds) at birth. That is more than the average person weighs as an adult!

Earth's tallest babies are giraffes. How tall? They can peek over a five-foot fence from the day they are born!

▲ A baby giraffe can be more than five feet tall.

Built-in Baby Carrier

Some mammals carry their babies for months after they are born. How? They have special pouches, or bags, in their fur. These mammals are called marsupials.

A red kangaroo is a kind of marsupial. It is smaller than your little finger when it is born. It lives in a pouch in its mother's fur. The baby stays inside the pouch for six months. Then it sometimes leaves the pouch. A baby kangaroo can ride in its mother's pouch for up to nine months.

▶ **A young red kangaroo rides in its mother's pouch.**

▲ Laying hundreds of eggs helps fish survive.

More Are Better

Many kinds of animals lay many eggs at one time. Some fish and insects can lay hundreds. Why do they lay so many eggs?

Many of the eggs do not survive. Some are eaten. Some just die. But if there are many to start, then more may survive. For many kinds of animals, more eggs means a better chance that their young will live and grow.

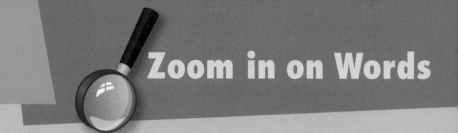
Many kinds of words are used in this book. Here you will learn about synonyms. You will also learn about antonyms.

Synonyms

Synonyms are words that have the same meanings. Find the synonyms in the sentences below.

The tiger life cycle **begins** again.

The praying mantis life cycle **starts** again.

The eggs look the **same.**

The nymphs look **alike.**

Antonyms

Antonyms are words that have opposite meanings. Find the antonyms in the sentences below.

The baby goat is **small.**

The adult goat is **large.**

This land is **wet.**

This land is **dry.**

This young arctic fox is **inside** the den.

This young arctic fox is **outside** the den.

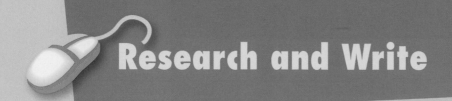

Research and Write

Write About a Life Cycle

Choose an animal to research. Find out about the animal's life cycle. Then write a report telling what you learned.

Research
Collect books and reference materials, or go online.

Read and Take Notes
As you read, take notes and draw pictures.

Write
Then write a report about the animal's life. Tell how it changes during its life cycle. Then draw a picture showing how the animal looks at each stage of its life cycle.

Read and Compare

Read More About Life Cycles

Find and read other books about animals. As you read, think about these questions.

- What do all life cycles have in common?
- How can life cycles be different?
- How do scientists learn about life cycles?

Books to Read

▲ Read about life cycles of many kinds of animals.

▲ Read about how scientists group kinds of animals.

▲ Read about animal features and behaviors.

Glossary

amphibian (page 10)
Animal that often lives part of its life on land and part in water
A salamander is an amphibian.

egg case (page 20)
A hard covering that protects eggs
Praying mantis eggs are in an egg case.

insect (page 12)
Animal that has six legs, three body parts, and a hard outer covering
A grasshopper is an insect.

larva (page 10)
An early stage in the life of an amphibian or other kind of animal
A salamander larva lives in water.

life cycle (page 7)
The stages an animal goes through during its life
A grasshopper has three stages in its life cycle.

mammal (page 8)
A kind of animal that has a backbone, feeds its young milk, and is usually covered with hair
A horse is a mammal.

mate (page 9)
To make babies
Adult praying mantises mate and have babies.

nymph (page 12)
A stage in the life of some insects between egg and adult
The dragonfly nymph does not have wings.

reptile (page 14)
Animal that has a backbone, scales, and uses the sun or warm surfaces to heat its body
A snake is a reptile.

Index